THE WORKBOOK FOR SMART GOALS

The scientifically proven template for successful goal setting

In the name of the most beneficent and merciful God, I write this book in hope that it may help people reach goals that are good and noble. I am aware that without the help of God nothing has ever been achieved nor can ever be attained. So I hope and pray for help and guidance for me and those reading this book.

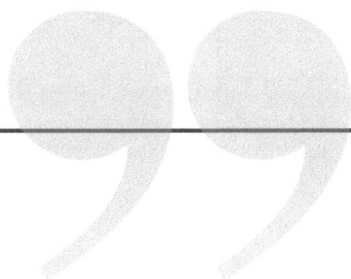

A goal,
properly set,
is halfway
reached.

WHAT ARE SMART GOALS?

SMART is an acronym that stands for **Specific, Measurable, Achievable, Relevant,** and **Timely.**

Many people set goals that are too vague like *"I want to be healthier"*. Such resolutions are not only hard to follow through but one can't know when the goal has been reached. The principal advantage of **SMART** objectives is that it is easier to know and understand when they have been done. Multiple studies show that SMART goals are central to planning and attaining effective changes. The question is, how to turn your goals into SMART goals?

HOW TO TURN YOUR GOALS INTO SMART GOALS?

Let's look at a simple example - *"I want to get in shape"*.

This is a typical way of framing goals, but it is too vague and has very little possibility of actually being fulfilled. Now let's try to reframe it using the **SMART formula**.

Specific

S When setting a goal, try to be as specific as possible. This isn't a detailed list of how you will achieve the goal, but it should answer as many questions as possible, like - What? Which? Why? Where? Etc

What do you want to accomplish? Who needs to be included? When do you want to do this? Why is this goal great?

In the given example, a specific statement may be arrived at like this -

"I will lose 15 pounds to get to my ideal weight."

Measurable

M How are you going to measure your goal? This makes the goal more tangible because it provides a way to measure progress.

In the above example, the goal can be easily measured by checking one's weight.

Achievable

A A goal is meant to inspire and motivate, not discourage. So in this step, think about what you'll need to achieve your goal and whether you have the required tools or skills. If not, you may try to think up ways to attain the skills or tools you need.

In this example, an assessment of attainability may go like this - *"I've done my research and found that 15 pounds can be lost healthily in 4 months through simple diet changes and exercise. I can join a gym to exercise regularly and visit a nutritionist to get advice on healthy ways to lose weight."*

Relevant

R This step focuses on determining whether your goal is in alignment with your vision and values. If not, how to make it so.

In this example - *"Losing weight to get in shape is in alignment with my overall life vision of looking and feeling good in my body."*

Timely

T Anyone can set goals, but without the urgency of a deadline, chances are high that it won't see fulfillment. Set a specific deadline and also milestones to be reached in between. So if a goal takes 6 months to finish, how much must be accomplished in the first month, the second month, and so on.

In our weight loss example, setting deadlines may look like this -

"I will lose 15 pounds before my wedding anniversary on 31 April 2022."

Thus, after brainstorming through all the aspects of SMART goals, the example goal of *" I want to get in shape"* can be reframed as

"I will weigh 109 pounds on 31 April 2022, by losing 15 pounds through diet and exercise."

<u>Your turn. What goals will you turn into SMART Goals today?</u>

SMART GOALS TEMPLATES

Use the questions as a guide to arrive at your own SMART goals

Original Goal

Specific
S
What do you want to accomplish? Who needs to work on it? Why is this a great goal?

Measurable
M
How will you track your progress? How will you know if you have reached your goal?

Achievable
A
How will you reach this goal? Do you have the skills or resources needed to achieve the results you seek? If not, how can you acquire the necessary skills or resources?

Relevant

R

Is this goal relevant to your life now? How does it align with the rest of your life and values?

Timely

T

What is the final deadline? Are there periodic deadlines for the different action steps you need to reach this goal?

New SMART Goal

Review and summarize what you have written above to create your new SMART goal.

Original Goal

Specific

S

What do you want to accomplish? Who needs to work on it? Why is this a great goal?

Measurable

M

How will you track your progress? How will you know if you have reached your goal?

Achievable

A

How will you reach this goal? Do you have the skills or resources needed to achieve the results you seek? If not, how can you acquire the necessary skills or resources?

Relevant

R

Is this goal relevant to your life now? How does it align with the rest of your life and values?

Timely

T

What is the final deadline? Are there periodic deadlines for the different action steps you need to reach this goal?

New SMART Goal

Review and summarize what you have written above to create your new SMART goal.

Original Goal

Specific
S

What do you want to accomplish? Who needs to work on it? Why is this a great goal?

Measurable
M

How will you track your progress? How will you know if you have reached your goal?

Achievable
A

How will you reach this goal? Do you have the skills or resources needed to achieve the results you seek? If not, how can you acquire the necessary skills or resources?

Relevant

R

Is this goal relevant to your life now? How does it align with the rest of your life and values?

Timely

T

What is the final deadline? Are there periodic deadlines for the different action steps you need to reach this goal?

New SMART Goal

Review and summarize what you have written above to create your new SMART goal.

Original Goal

Specific

S

What do you want to accomplish? Who needs to work on it? Why is this a great goal?

Measurable

M

How will you track your progress? How will you know if you have reached your goal?

Achievable

A

How will you reach this goal? Do you have the skills or resources needed to achieve the results you seek? If not, how can you acquire the necessary skills or resources?

Relevant

R

Is this goal relevant to your life now? How does it align with the rest of your life and values?

Timely

T

What is the final deadline? Are there periodic deadlines for the different action steps you need to reach this goal?

New SMART Goal

Review and summarize what you have written above to create your new SMART goal.

Original Goal

Specific

S

What do you want to accomplish? Who needs to work on it? Why is this a great goal?

Measurable

M

How will you track your progress? How will you know if you have reached your goal?

Achievable

A

How will you reach this goal? Do you have the skills or resources needed to achieve the results you seek? If not, how can you acquire the necessary skills or resources?

Relevant

R

Is this goal relevant to your life now? How does it align with the rest of your life and values?

Timely

T

What is the final deadline? Are there periodic deadlines for the different action steps you need to reach this goal?

New SMART Goal

Review and summarize what you have written above to create your new SMART goal.

Original Goal

Specific

S

What do you want to accomplish? Who needs to work on it? Why is this a great goal?

Measurable

M

How will you track your progress? How will you know if you have reached your goal?

Achievable

A

How will you reach this goal? Do you have the skills or resources needed to achieve the results you seek? If not, how can you acquire the necessary skills or resources?

Relevant

R

Is this goal relevant to your life now? How does it align with the rest of your life and values?

Timely

T

What is the final deadline? Are there periodic deadlines for the different action steps you need to reach this goal?

New SMART Goal

Review and summarize what you have written above to create your new SMART goal.

Original Goal

Specific
S
What do you want to accomplish? Who needs to work on it? Why is this a great goal?

Measurable
M
How will you track your progress? How will you know if you have reached your goal?

Achievable
A
How will you reach this goal? Do you have the skills or resources needed to achieve the results you seek? If not, how can you acquire the necessary skills or resources?

Relevant

R

Is this goal relevant to your life now? How does it align with the rest of your life and values?

Timely

T

What is the final deadline? Are there periodic deadlines for the different action steps you need to reach this goal?

New SMART Goal

Review and summarize what you have written above to create your new SMART goal.

Original Goal

Specific

S

What do you want to accomplish? Who needs to work on it? Why is this a great goal?

Measurable

M

How will you track your progress? How will you know if you have reached your goal?

Achievable

A

How will you reach this goal? Do you have the skills or resources needed to achieve the results you seek? If not, how can you acquire the necessary skills or resources?

Relevant

R

Is this goal relevant to your life now? How does it align with the rest of your life and values?

Timely

T

What is the final deadline? Are there periodic deadlines for the different action steps you need to reach this goal?

New SMART Goal

Review and summarize what you have written above to create your new SMART goal.

Original Goal

Specific

S

What do you want to accomplish? Who needs to work on it? Why is this a great goal?

Measurable

M

How will you track your progress? How will you know if you have reached your goal?

Achievable

A

How will you reach this goal? Do you have the skills or resources needed to achieve the results you seek? If not, how can you acquire the necessary skills or resources?

Relevant

R

Is this goal relevant to your life now? How does it align with the rest of your life and values?

Timely

T

What is the final deadline? Are there periodic deadlines for the different action steps you need to reach this goal?

New SMART Goal

Review and summarize what you have written above to create your new SMART goal.

Original Goal

Specific
S

What do you want to accomplish? Who needs to work on it? Why is this a great goal?

Measurable
M

How will you track your progress? How will you know if you have reached your goal?

Achievable
A

How will you reach this goal? Do you have the skills or resources needed to achieve the results you seek? If not, how can you acquire the necessary skills or resources?

Relevant

R

Is this goal relevant to your life now? How does it align with the rest of your life and values?

Timely

T

What is the final deadline? Are there periodic deadlines for the different action steps you need to reach this goal?

New SMART Goal

Review and summarize what you have written above to create your new SMART goal.

Original Goal

Specific

S

What do you want to accomplish? Who needs to work on it? Why is this a great goal?

Measurable

M

How will you track your progress? How will you know if you have reached your goal?

Achievable

A

How will you reach this goal? Do you have the skills or resources needed to achieve the results you seek? If not, how can you acquire the necessary skills or resources?

Relevant

R

Is this goal relevant to your life now? How does it align with the rest of your life and values?

Timely

T

What is the final deadline? Are there periodic deadlines for the different action steps you need to reach this goal?

New SMART Goal

Review and summarize what you have written above to create your new SMART goal.

Original Goal

Specific
S

What do you want to accomplish? Who needs to work on it? Why is this a great goal?

Measurable
M

How will you track your progress? How will you know if you have reached your goal?

Achievable
A

How will you reach this goal? Do you have the skills or resources needed to achieve the results you seek? If not, how can you acquire the necessary skills or resources?

Relevant

R

Is this goal relevant to your life now? How does it align with the rest of your life and values?

Timely

T

What is the final deadline? Are there periodic deadlines for the different action steps you need to reach this goal?

New SMART Goal

Review and summarize what you have written above to create your new SMART goal.

Original Goal

Specific
S
What do you want to accomplish? Who needs to work on it? Why is this a great goal?

Measurable
M
How will you track your progress? How will you know if you have reached your goal?

Achievable
A
How will you reach this goal? Do you have the skills or resources needed to achieve the results you seek? If not, how can you acquire the necessary skills or resources?

Relevant

Is this goal relevant to your life now? How does it align with the rest of your life and values?

R

Timely

What is the final deadline? Are there periodic deadlines for the different action steps you need to reach this goal?

T

New SMART Goal

Review and summarize what you have written above to create your new SMART goal.

Original Goal

Specific

S

What do you want to accomplish? Who needs to work on it? Why is this a great goal?

Measurable

M

How will you track your progress? How will you know if you have reached your goal?

Achievable

A

How will you reach this goal? Do you have the skills or resources needed to achieve the results you seek? If not, how can you acquire the necessary skills or resources?

Relevant

R

Is this goal relevant to your life now? How does it align with the rest of your life and values?

Timely

T

What is the final deadline? Are there periodic deadlines for the different action steps you need to reach this goal?

New SMART Goal

Review and summarize what you have written above to create your new SMART goal.

Original Goal

Specific

S

What do you want to accomplish? Who needs to work on it? Why is this a great goal?

Measurable

M

How will you track your progress? How will you know if you have reached your goal?

Achievable

A

How will you reach this goal? Do you have the skills or resources needed to achieve the results you seek? If not, how can you acquire the necessary skills or resources?

Relevant

Is this goal relevant to your life now? How does it align with the rest of your life and values?

R

Timely

What is the final deadline? Are there periodic deadlines for the different action steps you need to reach this goal?

T

New SMART Goal

Review and summarize what you have written above to create your new SMART goal.

Original Goal

Specific
S

What do you want to accomplish? Who needs to work on it? Why is this a great goal?

Measurable
M

How will you track your progress? How will you know if you have reached your goal?

Achievable
A

How will you reach this goal? Do you have the skills or resources needed to achieve the results you seek? If not, how can you acquire the necessary skills or resources?

Relevant

R

Is this goal relevant to your life now? How does it align with the rest of your life and values?

Timely

T

What is the final deadline? Are there periodic deadlines for the different action steps you need to reach this goal?

New SMART Goal

Review and summarize what you have written above to create your new SMART goal.

Original Goal

Specific

S

What do you want to accomplish? Who needs to work on it? Why is this a great goal?

Measurable

M

How will you track your progress? How will you know if you have reached your goal?

Achievable

A

How will you reach this goal? Do you have the skills or resources needed to achieve the results you seek? If not, how can you acquire the necessary skills or resources?

Relevant

R

Is this goal relevant to your life now? How does it align with the rest of your life and values?

Timely

T

What is the final deadline? Are there periodic deadlines for the different action steps you need to reach this goal?

New SMART Goal

Review and summarize what you have written above to create your new SMART goal.

Original Goal

Specific

S

What do you want to accomplish? Who needs to work on it? Why is this a great goal?

Measurable

M

How will you track your progress? How will you know if you have reached your goal?

Achievable

A

How will you reach this goal? Do you have the skills or resources needed to achieve the results you seek? If not, how can you acquire the necessary skills or resources?

Relevant

R

Is this goal relevant to your life now? How does it align with the rest of your life and values?

Timely

T

What is the final deadline? Are there periodic deadlines for the different action steps you need to reach this goal?

New SMART Goal

Review and summarize what you have written above to create your new SMART goal.

Original Goal

Specific

S

What do you want to accomplish? Who needs to work on it? Why is this a great goal?

Measurable

M

How will you track your progress? How will you know if you have reached your goal?

Achievable

A

How will you reach this goal? Do you have the skills or resources needed to achieve the results you seek? If not, how can you acquire the necessary skills or resources?

Relevant

R

Is this goal relevant to your life now? How does it align with the rest of your life and values?

Timely

T

What is the final deadline? Are there periodic deadlines for the different action steps you need to reach this goal?

New SMART Goal

Review and summarize what you have written above to create your new SMART goal.

Original Goal

Specific

S

What do you want to accomplish? Who needs to work on it? Why is this a great goal?

Measurable

M

How will you track your progress? How will you know if you have reached your goal?

Achievable

A

How will you reach this goal? Do you have the skills or resources needed to achieve the results you seek? If not, how can you acquire the necessary skills or resources?

Relevant

R

Is this goal relevant to your life now? How does it align with the rest of your life and values?

Timely

T

What is the final deadline? Are there periodic deadlines for the different action steps you need to reach this goal?

New SMART Goal

Review and summarize what you have written above to create your new SMART goal.

Original Goal

Specific

S

What do you want to accomplish? Who needs to work on it? Why is this a great goal?

Measurable

M

How will you track your progress? How will you know if you have reached your goal?

Achievable

A

How will you reach this goal? Do you have the skills or resources needed to achieve the results you seek? If not, how can you acquire the necessary skills or resources?

Relevant

R

Is this goal relevant to your life now? How does it align with the rest of your life and values?

Timely

T

What is the final deadline? Are there periodic deadlines for the different action steps you need to reach this goal?

New SMART Goal

Review and summarize what you have written above to create your new SMART goal.

Original Goal

Specific

S

What do you want to accomplish? Who needs to work on it? Why is this a great goal?

Measurable

M

How will you track your progress? How will you know if you have reached your goal?

Achievable

A

How will you reach this goal? Do you have the skills or resources needed to achieve the results you seek? If not, how can you acquire the necessary skills or resources?

Relevant

R

Is this goal relevant to your life now? How does it align with the rest of your life and values?

Timely

T

What is the final deadline? Are there periodic deadlines for the different action steps you need to reach this goal?

New
SMART
Goal

Review and summarize what you have written above to create your new SMART goal.

Original Goal

Specific

S

What do you want to accomplish? Who needs to work on it? Why is this a great goal?

Measurable

M

How will you track your progress? How will you know if you have reached your goal?

Achievable

A

How will you reach this goal? Do you have the skills or resources needed to achieve the results you seek? If not, how can you acquire the necessary skills or resources?

Relevant

R

Is this goal relevant to your life now? How does it align with the rest of your life and values?

Timely

T

What is the final deadline? Are there periodic deadlines for the different action steps you need to reach this goal?

New SMART Goal

Review and summarize what you have written above to create your new SMART goal.

Original Goal

Specific

S

What do you want to accomplish? Who needs to work on it? Why is this a great goal?

Measurable

M

How will you track your progress? How will you know if you have reached your goal?

Achievable

A

How will you reach this goal? Do you have the skills or resources needed to achieve the results you seek? If not, how can you acquire the necessary skills or resources?

Relevant

R

Is this goal relevant to your life now? How does it align with the rest of your life and values?

Timely

T

What is the final deadline? Are there periodic deadlines for the different action steps you need to reach this goal?

New SMART Goal

Review and summarize what you have written above to create your new SMART goal.

Original Goal

Specific

S

What do you want to accomplish? Who needs to work on it? Why is this a great goal?

Measurable

M

How will you track your progress? How will you know if you have reached your goal?

Achievable

A

How will you reach this goal? Do you have the skills or resources needed to achieve the results you seek? If not, how can you acquire the necessary skills or resources?

Relevant

R

Is this goal relevant to your life now? How does it align with the rest of your life and values?

Timely

T

What is the final deadline? Are there periodic deadlines for the different action steps you need to reach this goal?

New SMART Goal

Review and summarize what you have written above to create your new SMART goal.

Original Goal

Specific

S

What do you want to accomplish? Who needs to work on it? Why is this a great goal?

Measurable

M

How will you track your progress? How will you know if you have reached your goal?

Achievable

A

How will you reach this goal? Do you have the skills or resources needed to achieve the results you seek? If not, how can you acquire the necessary skills or resources?

Relevant

R

Is this goal relevant to your life now? How does it align with the rest of your life and values?

Timely

T

What is the final deadline? Are there periodic deadlines for the different action steps you need to reach this goal?

New SMART Goal

Review and summarize what you have written above to create your new SMART goal.

Original Goal

Specific

S

What do you want to accomplish? Who needs to work on it? Why is this a great goal?

Measurable

M

How will you track your progress? How will you know if you have reached your goal?

Achievable

A

How will you reach this goal? Do you have the skills or resources needed to achieve the results you seek? If not, how can you acquire the necessary skills or resources?

Relevant

R

Is this goal relevant to your life now? How does it align with the rest of your life and values?

Timely

T

What is the final deadline? Are there periodic deadlines for the different action steps you need to reach this goal?

New SMART Goal

Review and summarize what you have written above to create your new SMART goal.

Original Goal

Specific

S

What do you want to accomplish? Who needs to work on it? Why is this a great goal?

Measurable

M

How will you track your progress? How will you know if you have reached your goal?

Achievable

A

How will you reach this goal? Do you have the skills or resources needed to achieve the results you seek? If not, how can you acquire the necessary skills or resources?

Relevant

R

Is this goal relevant to your life now? How does it align with the rest of your life and values?

Timely

T

What is the final deadline? Are there periodic deadlines for the different action steps you need to reach this goal?

New SMART Goal

Review and summarize what you have written above to create your new SMART goal.

Original Goal

Specific
S
What do you want to accomplish? Who needs to work on it? Why is this a great goal?

Measurable
M
How will you track your progress? How will you know if you have reached your goal?

Achievable
A
How will you reach this goal? Do you have the skills or resources needed to achieve the results you seek? If not, how can you acquire the necessary skills or resources?

Relevant

Is this goal relevant to your life now? How does it align with the rest of your life and values?

R

Timely

What is the final deadline? Are there periodic deadlines for the different action steps you need to reach this goal?

T

New SMART Goal

Review and summarize what you have written above to create your new SMART goal.

Original Goal

Specific

S

What do you want to accomplish? Who needs to work on it? Why is this a great goal?

Measurable

M

How will you track your progress? How will you know if you have reached your goal?

Achievable

A

How will you reach this goal? Do you have the skills or resources needed to achieve the results you seek? If not, how can you acquire the necessary skills or resources?

Relevant

R

Is this goal relevant to your life now? How does it align with the rest of your life and values?

Timely

T

What is the final deadline? Are there periodic deadlines for the different action steps you need to reach this goal?

New SMART Goal

Review and summarize what you have written above to create your new SMART goal.

Original Goal

Specific

S

What do you want to accomplish? Who needs to work on it? Why is this a great goal?

Measurable

M

How will you track your progress? How will you know if you have reached your goal?

Achievable

A

How will you reach this goal? Do you have the skills or resources needed to achieve the results you seek? If not, how can you acquire the necessary skills or resources?

Relevant

Is this goal relevant to your life now? How does it align with the rest of your life and values?

R

Timely

What is the final deadline? Are there periodic deadlines for the different action steps you need to reach this goal?

T

New SMART Goal

Review and summarize what you have written above to create your new SMART goal.

Original Goal

Specific

S

What do you want to accomplish? Who needs to work on it? Why is this a great goal?

Measurable

M

How will you track your progress? How will you know if you have reached your goal?

Achievable

A

How will you reach this goal? Do you have the skills or resources needed to achieve the results you seek? If not, how can you acquire the necessary skills or resources?

Relevant

R

Is this goal relevant to your life now? How does it align with the rest of your life and values?

Timely

T

What is the final deadline? Are there periodic deadlines for the different action steps you need to reach this goal?

New SMART Goal

Review and summarize what you have written above to create your new SMART goal.

Original Goal

Specific

S

What do you want to accomplish? Who needs to work on it? Why is this a great goal?

Measurable

M

How will you track your progress? How will you know if you have reached your goal?

Achievable

A

How will you reach this goal? Do you have the skills or resources needed to achieve the results you seek? If not, how can you acquire the necessary skills or resources?

Relevant

R

Is this goal relevant to your life now? How does it align with the rest of your life and values?

Timely

T

What is the final deadline? Are there periodic deadlines for the different action steps you need to reach this goal?

New SMART Goal

Review and summarize what you have written above to create your new SMART goal.

Original Goal

Specific

S

What do you want to accomplish? Who needs to work on it? Why is this a great goal?

Measurable

M

How will you track your progress? How will you know if you have reached your goal?

Achievable

A

How will you reach this goal? Do you have the skills or resources needed to achieve the results you seek? If not, how can you acquire the necessary skills or resources?

Relevant

R

Is this goal relevant to your life now? How does it align with the rest of your life and values?

Timely

T

What is the final deadline? Are there periodic deadlines for the different action steps you need to reach this goal?

New SMART Goal

Review and summarize what you have written above to create your new SMART goal.

Original Goal

Specific

S

What do you want to accomplish? Who needs to work on it? Why is this a great goal?

Measurable

M

How will you track your progress? How will you know if you have reached your goal?

Achievable

A

How will you reach this goal? Do you have the skills or resources needed to achieve the results you seek? If not, how can you acquire the necessary skills or resources?

Relevant

R

Is this goal relevant to your life now? How does it align with the rest of your life and values?

Timely

T

What is the final deadline? Are there periodic deadlines for the different action steps you need to reach this goal?

New SMART Goal

Review and summarize what you have written above to create your new SMART goal.

Original Goal

Specific

S

What do you want to accomplish? Who needs to work on it? Why is this a great goal?

Measurable

M

How will you track your progress? How will you know if you have reached your goal?

Achievable

A

How will you reach this goal? Do you have the skills or resources needed to achieve the results you seek? If not, how can you acquire the necessary skills or resources?

Relevant

R

Is this goal relevant to your life now? How does it align with the rest of your life and values?

Timely

T

What is the final deadline? Are there periodic deadlines for the different action steps you need to reach this goal?

New SMART Goal

Review and summarize what you have written above to create your new SMART goal.

Original Goal

Specific

S

What do you want to accomplish? Who needs to work on it? Why is this a great goal?

Measurable

M

How will you track your progress? How will you know if you have reached your goal?

Achievable

A

How will you reach this goal? Do you have the skills or resources needed to achieve the results you seek? If not, how can you acquire the necessary skills or resources?

Relevant

R

Is this goal relevant to your life now? How does it align with the rest of your life and values?

Timely

T

What is the final deadline? Are there periodic deadlines for the different action steps you need to reach this goal?

New SMART Goal

Review and summarize what you have written above to create your new SMART goal.

Original Goal

Specific

S

What do you want to accomplish? Who needs to work on it? Why is this a great goal?

Measurable

M

How will you track your progress? How will you know if you have reached your goal?

Achievable

A

How will you reach this goal? Do you have the skills or resources needed to achieve the results you seek? If not, how can you acquire the necessary skills or resources?

Relevant

R

Is this goal relevant to your life now? How does it align with the rest of your life and values?

Timely

T

What is the final deadline? Are there periodic deadlines for the different action steps you need to reach this goal?

New SMART Goal

Review and summarize what you have written above to create your new SMART goal.

Original Goal

Specific

S

What do you want to accomplish? Who needs to work on it? Why is this a great goal?

Measurable

M

How will you track your progress? How will you know if you have reached your goal?

Achievable

A

How will you reach this goal? Do you have the skills or resources needed to achieve the results you seek? If not, how can you acquire the necessary skills or resources?

Relevant

Is this goal relevant to your life now? How does it align with the rest of your life and values?

R

Timely

What is the final deadline? Are there periodic deadlines for the different action steps you need to reach this goal?

T

New SMART Goal

Review and summarize what you have written above to create your new SMART goal.

Original Goal

Specific
S

What do you want to accomplish? Who needs to work on it? Why is this a great goal?

Measurable
M

How will you track your progress? How will you know if you have reached your goal?

Achievable
A

How will you reach this goal? Do you have the skills or resources needed to achieve the results you seek? If not, how can you acquire the necessary skills or resources?

Relevant

Is this goal relevant to your life now? How does it align with the rest of your life and values?

R

Timely

What is the final deadline? Are there periodic deadlines for the different action steps you need to reach this goal?

T

New SMART Goal

Review and summarize what you have written above to create your new SMART goal.

Original Goal

Specific

S

What do you want to accomplish? Who needs to work on it? Why is this a great goal?

Measurable

M

How will you track your progress? How will you know if you have reached your goal?

Achievable

A

How will you reach this goal? Do you have the skills or resources needed to achieve the results you seek? If not, how can you acquire the necessary skills or resources?

Relevant

R

Is this goal relevant to your life now? How does it align with the rest of your life and values?

Timely

T

What is the final deadline? Are there periodic deadlines for the different action steps you need to reach this goal?

New SMART Goal

Review and summarize what you have written above to create your new SMART goal.

Original Goal

Specific

S

What do you want to accomplish? Who needs to work on it? Why is this a great goal?

Measurable

M

How will you track your progress? How will you know if you have reached your goal?

Achievable

A

How will you reach this goal? Do you have the skills or resources needed to achieve the results you seek? If not, how can you acquire the necessary skills or resources?

Relevant

R

Is this goal relevant to your life now? How does it align with the rest of your life and values?

Timely

T

What is the final deadline? Are there periodic deadlines for the different action steps you need to reach this goal?

New SMART Goal

Review and summarize what you have written above to create your new SMART goal.

Original Goal

Specific

S

What do you want to accomplish? Who needs to work on it? Why is this a great goal?

Measurable

M

How will you track your progress? How will you know if you have reached your goal?

Achievable

A

How will you reach this goal? Do you have the skills or resources needed to achieve the results you seek? If not, how can you acquire the necessary skills or resources?

Relevant

R

Is this goal relevant to your life now? How does it align with the rest of your life and values?

Timely

T

What is the final deadline? Are there periodic deadlines for the different action steps you need to reach this goal?

New SMART Goal

Review and summarize what you have written above to create your new SMART goal.

Original Goal

Specific

S

What do you want to accomplish? Who needs to work on it? Why is this a great goal?

Measurable

M

How will you track your progress? How will you know if you have reached your goal?

Achievable

A

How will you reach this goal? Do you have the skills or resources needed to achieve the results you seek? If not, how can you acquire the necessary skills or resources?

Relevant

Is this goal relevant to your life now? How does it align with the rest of your life and values?

R

Timely

What is the final deadline? Are there periodic deadlines for the different action steps you need to reach this goal?

T

New SMART Goal

Review and summarize what you have written above to create your new SMART goal.

Original Goal

Specific
S

What do you want to accomplish? Who needs to work on it? Why is this a great goal?

Measurable
M

How will you track your progress? How will you know if you have reached your goal?

Achievable
A

How will you reach this goal? Do you have the skills or resources needed to achieve the results you seek? If not, how can you acquire the necessary skills or resources?

Relevant

R

Is this goal relevant to your life now? How does it align with the rest of your life and values?

Timely

T

What is the final deadline? Are there periodic deadlines for the different action steps you need to reach this goal?

New SMART Goal

Review and summarize what you have written above to create your new SMART goal.

FREE RESOURCES

Thank you for using the workbook. If you liked it, you'll surely love the "Make it Happen" ebook. Scan the QR code to read the book and be the first ones who are informed of the latest updates and free resources.

Scan this code to download free printables of the SMART goals template to print out unlimited copies and set unlimited goals.

Made in United States
Troutdale, OR
09/23/2024

23083417R00056